# INSIGHT at Work

*Small Decisions*
*That Shape Remarkable Careers*

BY

LANRE B. OLALEYE

Published by LBO Publishing,
ISBN 979-8-9958150-0-6

# Table of Contents

# Dedication

*For every professional who shows up,*
*Keeps going, and quietly refuses to stop growing.*
Wherever you are. Whatever the conditions.
This book was written for you.

# ACKNOWLEDGEMENTS

## This book did not begin at a desk.

It began in rooms. In conversations. In the quiet after a meeting where something was said that I could not stop thinking about. In a mentor's office, a colleague's offhand remark, a classroom long ago where a teacher said something that landed differently than they probably intended.

To every person whose path has crossed mine since I began my working life — in every organisation, every team, every project, every conversation at the edge of a conference room or across a table or on the other end of a call — this book carries something of you in it. You may not recognise your specific contribution. But it is there.

To the mentors who saw more in me than I could see in myself at the time, and who said so when it mattered: I have tried to pass that forward in everything I write. The chapters in this book that speak about courage, about identity, about the long game — those chapters exist because someone, at a formative moment, chose to invest in a person who was still becoming.

To the teachers who understood that teaching is not the transfer of information but the expansion of what a person believes is possible for themselves: I have not forgotten you. The best of what is in these pages is an attempt to do for a reader what the best of you did for me.

To the colleagues who modelled excellence quietly, without asking for recognition — who simply did the work well, consistently, and let that speak: you are the reason Chapter 13 exists. I have watched you. I have learned from you more than I ever told you.

To the friends who stayed through the seasons when the work was slow and the direction was unclear — who asked the right questions and declined to offer easy reassurance when honest challenge was what was needed: you know who you are, and you know what those conversations cost you and gave me.

And to the readers of Insight with LBO — the professionals across the world who engaged with those early posts, who replied with their own stories, who asked the questions that became the chapters: this book is the answer I kept trying to give you. Your response to those LinkedIn posts told me that the conversation was bigger than I had imagined, and that it deserved something more considered than a series of posts could hold.

The world of work is changing faster than any single generation has had to absorb. The professionals navigating that change — building careers in conditions their parents could not have anticipated, trying to contribute meaningfully in organisations that are themselves still working out what they need to become — deserve more than advice. They deserve to be taken seriously.

**This book is an attempt to take them seriously.**

I am grateful to every person who contributed to it — knowingly or not.

The race to contribute meaningfully to humanity, and to set the next generation up for successful living, is one no single person runs alone.

# A NOTE
# ON THIS BOOK

## This is not a book about working harder.

It is a book about working with more intention — more clarity about who you are becoming, more consistency in how you show up, and a longer view of what a working life is actually for.

The ideas in these pages grew out of years of observation — watching talented professionals underperform not because they lacked ability, but because they lacked direction. Watching capable people mistake busyness for progress and effort for excellence. Watching others, with no obvious advantage in talent or opportunity, build careers of unusual depth and quiet influence — simply because they had learned to think differently about the work.

Those observations became the "Insight with LBO" series. The series became this book.

Each chapter is short. The language is direct. But do not let either of those things suggest that what is being asked of you is small. Reading is the easy part. The harder part — and the more valuable part — is the honest self-examination each chapter invites.

You do not need to be at the start of your career for this book to be useful. You do not need to be in crisis, or at a crossroads, or already certain that something needs to change. You need only to be someone who takes their work seriously — and who suspects, even slightly, that there is a more intentional version of the professional you are capable of becoming.

**If that is you, read slowly.**

Write in the margins. Return to the chapters that unsettled you. Let the questions sit before you reach for the answers.

The long game is not won in a single reading.

**It is won in the decisions that follow.**

## INTRODUCTION

# BEFORE YOU BEGIN

Somewhere in the middle of a career, something shifts.

Not dramatically. Not with a sudden crisis or a defining moment you can point to later. It happens quietly, over weeks and months, until one ordinary Tuesday you sit back and realise: you have been working hard for a long time, and you are not sure it is working.

You are not failing. You are not lazy. You are showing up, putting in the hours, saying yes to the right things.

And still, something feels misaligned.

The gap between capability and progress is rarely a talent gap.

It is a clarity gap. A direction gap. A gap between the effort you are putting in and the understanding of what that effort is building toward.

**If you feel that gap — if you suspect there is a more intentional version of the professional you are capable of becoming — this book was written for you.**

### Who This Book Is For

This book is written for professionals at any stage of their career who suspect there is a gap between the effort they are putting in and the progress they are seeing.

**If you are early in your career** — doing everything you have been told to do but finding that effort alone does not seem to be enough — this book will help you understand why activity and progress are not the same thing, and how to close the gap between them.

**If you are mid-career** — competent, respected, delivering results, but quietly wondering why the next level feels harder to reach than it should — this book will help you see what capable professionals often miss: that the internal foundations of clarity, consistency, and identity are what separate those who plateau from those who keep growing.

**If you lead others** — and you watch talented people struggle not because they lack ability but because they haven't yet built the clarity and direction they need — this book will give you the language and the framework to help them build what you cannot simply give them: a clearer sense of who they are becoming and how to sustain it.

This book does not require you to be in crisis. It does not require you to be at a crossroads. It requires only that you take your work seriously enough to examine it honestly — and that you are willing to do the harder, slower work of becoming more intentional about who you are, how you show up, and what kind of career you are building across the long arc of a working life.

## Why I Wrote This

I did not set out to write a book.

I set out to be useful.

The "Insight with LBO" series on LinkedIn began as a simple commitment: to share, each week, one idea that might help someone think more clearly about their work and their direction. Not theory. Not inspiration. Practical wisdom — the kind that is earned through observation, reflection, and years of watching what actually works.

What I did not anticipate was the response.

Week after week, readers wrote back. Not to debate the ideas, but to say: *this is exactly what I needed to hear.* A project manager in her third year. A director navigating a difficult transition. A founder building something new and feeling pulled in every direction. A young professional who had just been passed over for a promotion he had worked hard for.

Different people. Different stages. The same underlying struggle.

They were not struggling because they lacked ambition or ability. They were struggling because no one had ever helped them get clear — about who they were becoming, how they showed up, what they were truly capable of, and how to sustain it over time.

**That is the gap this book is written to fill.**

## What This Book Is — and What It Is Not

There are many excellent books about productivity, habits, and success. Some of them you have already read. You may have highlighted passages, completed the exercises, and felt a genuine surge of clarity when you finished.

And then, a few weeks later, the clarity faded.

This book is not a system. It is not a productivity framework or a step-by-step formula for professional success. It will not ask you to overhaul your morning routine or measure your habits with a spreadsheet.

What it will do is slower and, I believe, more lasting.

It will help you think differently — about how you work, how you grow, and how you sustain meaningful progress over the long arc of a career. Each chapter is short by design. The ideas are deliberately accessible. But accessible does not mean shallow. Every chapter asks something of you.

The difference between this book and the others on your shelf is this: those books tell you what to do. This one helps you understand who to *become.*

Behaviour without identity does not last. Systems without self-knowledge break down. This book works from the inside out.

## How the Book Is Structured

The book is built around four interconnected pillars. Together, they form the architecture of sustainable professional growth.

| | |
|---|---|
| **Section I**<br>**Clarity** | **How You Think**<br>Chapters 1–4. Clarity, purpose, mindset, and identity. The internal foundation everything else is built upon. |
| **Section II**<br>**Consistency** | **How You Show Up**<br>Chapters 5–7. Consistency, discipline, and small wins. How reliable daily behaviour builds unshakeable credibility. |
| **Section III**<br>**Capability** | **How You Grow**<br>Chapters 8–11. Learning, courage, preparation, and value. How to grow deliberately and make your contribution visible. |
| **Section IV**<br>**The Long Game** | **How You Sustain**<br>Chapters 12–15. Time, excellence, values, and finishing strong. How to play a career of depth, not just duration. |

The four sections are designed to build on each other. Clarity without consistency is wishful thinking. Consistency without capability plateaus. Capability without the long game burns out. Together, they form something integrated and lasting.

## How to Use This Book

This is not a book you need to read in one sitting, or even in order.

Some readers will move through it chapter by chapter, letting the ideas accumulate. Others will open it on a difficult morning, find the chapter that speaks to where they are, and sit with it for a while. Both approaches are right. The book was built to support either.

A few suggestions that will help you get the most from it:

**Read slowly.** Each chapter is short, but not meant to be rushed. Give ideas room to settle before moving to the next one.

**Use the Clarity Checkpoints.** Each chapter ends with a set of focused questions. Do not skip them. They are where the real work happens.

**Write your answers down.** Thinking in your head stays general. Writing makes it specific. A notebook kept alongside this book becomes a record of your growth.

**Return to chapters as seasons change.** A chapter that felt abstract in January may feel urgent in September. Your career will shift — let the book shift with it.

If you lead a team, consider working through a section together — one chapter per week, followed by a brief conversation. Clarity is contagious. When one person on a team gets clearer, the whole team feels it.

## A Word Before You Begin

I want to be honest with you about what this book can and cannot do.

It cannot replace the hard work of showing up, building skills, and navigating the complexity of real organisations and real relationships. No book can do that.

What it can do is give you a clearer lens. It can help you ask better questions about your work, your direction, and your habits — and better questions lead, over time, to better outcomes.

The professionals I have seen grow the most over their careers were not always the most talented people in the room. They were the ones who stayed clear about what mattered, showed up with consistency, kept growing when growth was uncomfortable, and played a long game when everyone around them was chasing a short one.

That is who this book is written for.

Not the loudest person in the room.

**The most intentional one.**

SECTION I

# CLARITY

*How You Think*

CHAPTER

# ONE

# THE POWER OF CLARITY

## It is 9:47 a.m on a Tuesday morning.

Marcus has been at his desk since 8:00 a.m. He has answered fourteen messages, joined two impromptu calls, reviewed a report he did not request, and been dragged into three decision-making meetings that were not his to make. His calendar shows six more meetings before 5:00 p.m.

He is not lazy. He is not disorganised. He is, by every visible measure, deeply busy.

And yet, by Friday afternoon, he will feel that the week produced almost nothing that mattered.

Not because the work was unimportant.

Because Marcus has no clarity about what *is* important — to him, in this season, right now.

**Clarity is often underestimated.**

In a world filled with information, speed, and endless options, clarity can feel slow — even unnecessary. Many people assume that effort alone will produce results, that motion will eventually lead to meaning, and that staying busy is the same as moving forward.

**It is not.**

Clarity is what turns effort into progress. Without it, even the most talented individuals can feel like Marcus — productive in motion, but empty in result.

When clarity is missing, everything feels urgent. Every request feels important. Every opportunity feels like something you must chase.

But when clarity is present, something shifts. Noise loses its grip. Distraction weakens. Decisions become lighter.

Clarity is not about having all the answers. It is about knowing what deserves your attention *now.*

## Why Clarity Comes Before Momentum

Many people believe momentum creates clarity. In reality, clarity creates momentum.

Think about the last time you sat down to work and genuinely knew what you needed to accomplish that day. Not a list of seventeen things — but one or two priorities that truly mattered. There was a different quality to that day. Energy moved in a direction instead of dispersing into noise.

That is the quiet power of clarity.

When you are clear about who you are, what you offer, and where you are going, energy stops leaking. You no longer spend mental effort debating every choice. You stop reacting to everything around you and begin responding intentionally.

**Clarity reduces friction.**

Instead of asking, "Should I do this?" you ask, "Does this align?" That single shift saves time, emotional energy, and focus — every single day.

## Clarity as a Decision Filter

Every day, work presents choices.

What to prioritise. What to postpone. What to say yes to. What to decline without guilt.

Without clarity, decisions feel heavy because they are made in isolation. Each choice is debated on its own merits, without reference to a larger picture. This is why professionals with full calendars can still feel paralysed by a single decision — the decision itself is not difficult. The absence of a guiding frame is.

Clarity provides that picture.

It acts as a filter — quietly guiding decisions before they become stressful. When purpose is clear, distraction loses its power. When direction is defined, urgency is put in its proper place.

Clarity does not eliminate complexity. It gives you a way to navigate it.

## The Emotional Weight of Unclear Work

A lack of clarity does more than slow progress. It drains motivation.

There is a particular kind of exhaustion that has nothing to do with hours worked. It belongs to people who worked hard all week but cannot point to what they built. Who said yes to everything and still feel they have let someone down. Who moved constantly but arrived nowhere.

That is the exhaustion of unclear work.

People in this state are often hardworking and capable, yet perpetually depleted. Not because the work is too demanding, but because the direction is uncertain. Effort without orientation is not discipline — it is survival.

**Clarity restores meaning.**

When you understand *why* your work matters and *how* it fits into a larger path, effort becomes purposeful again. Progress may still be slow, but it no longer feels empty.

## Clarity Is Built, Not Found

Here is what no one tells you about clarity: you cannot wait for it.

Most people treat clarity like weather — something that either arrives or doesn't, beyond their control. They wait for the right moment, the right opportunity, or a quiet week that never comes. Meanwhile, the work accumulates and the direction stays blurred.

Clarity is not something you stumble upon. It is something you build.

It is shaped through reflection, honest assessment, and intentional decision-making. It grows when you ask better questions and resist the pressure to move before thinking. It deepens as you:

- Define what matters in this season — not every season, this one.
- Understand your genuine strengths and your honest limits.
- Recognise what no longer serves the direction you are moving toward.

Over time, clarity becomes a steady companion — not a rare, lucky moment.

## Clarity Checkpoint

*Pause here. Answer these three questions without editing yourself:*

1. What am I actually trying to build right now?
2. What deserves my best energy this week?
3. What am I allowing out of habit rather than intention?

*You do not need perfect answers. You need honest ones. Clarity begins where honesty meets intention.*

## Closing Reflection

Marcus did not have a talent problem, a work ethic problem, or a time problem.

**He had a clarity problem.**

And clarity problems are solvable — not through more effort, but through more intention.

Clarity does not guarantee ease. But it guarantees direction.

In a world that rewards speed and visibility, clarity rewards patience and depth. It anchors you when the path feels crowded and reminds you that progress is not about doing everything — it is about doing the *right* things, consistently.

Clarity is not loud.

But it is powerful.

**And it is the foundation upon which meaningful work is built.**

CHAPTER

# TWO

## PURPOSE CREATES FOCUS

### Priya had seventeen tabs open.

Not unusual for a Wednesday. There was the quarterly report she had been drafting in fragments, three unanswered messages from her manager, a half-read article on leadership she had promised herself she would finish, two project files awaiting her review, and a calendar invite for a meeting she was not sure she needed to attend.

She had downloaded a new focus app the week before. She had also reorganised her task list, blocked two hours every morning as "deep work" time, and silenced all notifications before 10 a.m.

None of it was working.

The problem was not her tools or her schedule. The problem was that Priya did not have a clear answer to one question: *What am I actually here to do?*

Without that answer, every task felt equally urgent. Without that anchor, focus had nowhere to land.

**Focus is often treated as a productivity skill.**

People search for better tools, sharper techniques, and more aggressive systems. They silence notifications, restructure their mornings, and try to manage distraction as though it were an external intruder rather than a symptom of something internal.

But focus is not primarily a tactical problem.

**It is a purpose problem.**

When purpose is unclear, everything feels urgent. When purpose is understood, distraction loses its power — not because distractions disappear, but because they no longer compete on equal footing with what truly matters.

Purpose is not merely inspiration or passion. It is a stabilising force that brings order to attention.

## Why Focus Fails Without Purpose

Many professionals struggle with focus not because they lack discipline, but because they lack direction.

When you are unsure of what truly matters, every task competes for attention. Emails interrupt thinking. Meetings fragment energy. Requests feel impossible to decline, because without a guiding standard, there is no basis on which to decline them.

Over time, attention becomes scattered and effort diluted. Busyness increases while progress slows.

This is why better apps and tidier task lists rarely solve the problem. They organise the noise. They do not silence it.

**Purpose corrects this at the root.**

It clarifies what deserves your best energy and what does not. It gives focus a destination — somewhere specific to point toward rather than the general, exhausting direction of everywhere at once.

## Purpose as a Compass, Not a Goal

Purpose is often misunderstood as a distant end state — a grand vision to be achieved someday, once the conditions are right.

That misunderstanding keeps many capable people waiting.

In reality, purpose functions more like a compass than a finish line. It does not tell you exactly where you will arrive. It tells you which direction to move. And in a working life full of choices, options, and competing pressures, that is often exactly what is needed.

When purpose is clear, decisions become easier. You begin to evaluate opportunities not by urgency or pressure, but by alignment. The question shifts from *"Can I do this?"* to *"Should I?"*

That single shift — from capability to alignment — protects focus more reliably than any scheduling system ever could.

## The Freedom to Say No

One of the quietest benefits of purpose is permission.

Permission to decline without guilt. Permission to ignore what does not align. Permission to release expectations that no longer fit the season you are in.

For many professionals, saying no feels dangerous. It risks disappointing someone, appearing uncooperative, or missing an opportunity. And so they say yes — again, and again — until the calendar is full and the work that actually matters has been crowded out by the work that simply arrived.

Purpose changes the calculus entirely.

Without purpose, saying no feels risky.

**With purpose, saying no feels responsible.**

Focus is not about doing more. It is about doing what matters — and having the clarity to know the difference.

## Purpose Reduces Mental Fatigue

There is a particular kind of tiredness that sleep does not fix.

It comes from constant evaluation — from having to assess and re-assess every decision because there is no reliable internal framework to settle them quickly. When values and direction are unclear, every choice requires fresh energy. Every request demands a fresh debate. Over time, this creates an exhaustion that rest alone cannot fully resolve.

**Purpose simplifies thinking.**

When you know why you are working and what you are building, many decisions resolve themselves before they reach the level of conscious debate. Focus becomes less about willpower and more about alignment. Energy lasts longer because it is spent with intention rather than scattered across everything that demands it.

The professionals who seem inexhaustible are rarely working harder than everyone else. They are working in better alignment with what matters to them. That alignment is a form of efficiency no calendar can replicate.

## Purpose Grows Through Seasons

Purpose is not static.

It evolves as responsibilities deepen, opportunities expand, and life unfolds in directions you did not predict. What mattered most at twenty-eight may look different at thirty-eight. What drove you in your first leadership role may shift when you have held that role for a decade.

Clarity of purpose does not require lifelong certainty. It requires what I call **seasonal honesty** — the willingness to ask, in this season of your career and your life, what truly matters now.

Some professionals resist this question because they fear the answer will require difficult change. Others avoid it because they feel they should already know. But purpose that is never revisited becomes a story you tell about yourself rather than a direction you are actually moving in.

Purpose becomes powerful when you allow it to be revisited, refined, and renewed. Not constantly — restlessness is not clarity. But regularly enough that it remains honest.

## Clarity Checkpoint

*Complete this sentence without overthinking it:*

**"I help ________________ achieve ________________ through ____________."**

*This statement does not need to be permanent. It only needs to be true* ***now****.*

*Then ask yourself two more:*

1. What decision have I been avoiding that my purpose, stated clearly, would actually resolve?
2. What am I currently doing that no longer fits the answer I just wrote?

*Clarity of purpose grows when language becomes precise — and when honest answers are acted on.*

## Closing Reflection

Priya did not need a better app.

She needed a clearer answer to one question — and the discipline to let that answer guide her week.

Focus is not about force. It is about direction.

Purpose turns attention into intention. It transforms effort into meaning. When purpose is clear, work feels lighter — not because it is easier, but because it is aligned.

And aligned work sustains focus in ways that discipline alone never could.

You cannot organise your way to purpose.

**But with purpose, almost everything else begins to organise itself.**

CHAPTER

# THREE

## MINDSET SHAPES OUTCOME

Two colleagues received the same feedback on the same day.

Their manager told them both, directly, that their presentations needed work. The ideas were strong, but the delivery was losing the room. She recommended they invest in developing that skill.

The first colleague, Daniel, left the meeting quiet. By the end of the day, he had told two people that the manager simply did not understand his style. Within a week, he had mentally filed the feedback under "unfair" and moved on without changing anything.

The second colleague, Yvonne, left the same meeting uncomfortable — but curious. She booked time with a mentor that week. She watched recordings of effective presenters. She asked to present again at the next team session, not because she felt ready, but because she understood that readiness follows practice, not the other way around.

Same feedback. Same opportunity to grow.

**Entirely different outcomes.**

The difference was not talent. It was not opportunity. It was not even effort.

**It was mindset.**

**Mindset is the lens through which you interpret pressure, possibility, failure, and growth.**

It quietly shapes how you respond long before outcomes are visible. Two people can face the same situation — the same setback, the same opening, the same difficult conversation — and walk away with entirely different results. Not because the situation treated them differently, but because they interpreted it differently.

Change the lens, and the path changes.

## Why Outcomes Begin Internally

Many people try to change results without examining beliefs.

They adjust strategy, seek new environments, or wait for better circumstances. Each of those moves has merit. But they are rarely sufficient on their own, because the thinking that created the current results often travels with the person into the new situation.

**Outcomes are often the visible expression of invisible thinking.**

If you believe growth is possible, effort feels worthwhile. If you believe progress is unlikely, motivation fades quickly — often before the evidence is in. The mind reaches conclusions about what is possible, and then organises behaviour accordingly.

Belief influences behaviour. Behaviour shapes results.

This is why two equally talented professionals, given the same opportunity, can produce such different outcomes. The visible gap between them is in their results. The real gap is in what they believe about themselves.

## The Stories You Tell Yourself

Every professional carries an internal narrative.

Sometimes it is encouraging. More often, at least in the quiet moments, it is limiting.

These stories are familiar because they are almost universal:

> *"I'm not ready yet."*
>
> *"I don't know enough."*
>
> *"Others are more qualified."*
>
> *"It's too late for me to change direction."*

Left unchecked, these narratives do not just discourage. They govern. They determine which opportunities you pursue, which risks you avoid, and how long you persist when things get difficult. They become the quiet rules by which you live your professional life — even when no one imposed them on you.

Mindset is not just what you think.

**It is what you believe to be true about what is possible for you.**

## Thoughts as Seeds

Every thought grows into something.

Repeated thoughts take root. They form patterns. And those patterns influence confidence, courage, and consistency long before they produce any visible result.

This is worth sitting with, because it cuts both ways. The professional who tells themselves repeatedly that they are capable of handling more responsibility gradually builds the interior architecture to do exactly that. And the professional who tells themselves repeatedly that they are not the kind of person who gets promoted quietly reinforces the behaviours that make that story true.

**A healthy mindset does not deny reality. It interprets reality constructively.**

It allows you to acknowledge difficulty without surrendering to it. To see a setback as information rather than verdict. To recognise that most professional limitations are not fixed — they are simply current.

## When Skill Meets Mindset

Skill alone is not enough.

This is one of the more uncomfortable truths in professional development, because most people invest heavily in skills and relatively little in examining the beliefs that govern whether those skills are actually used.

Highly skilled individuals hesitate before important conversations because they do not believe they deserve to be heard. They procrastinate on high-visibility work because they fear that full effort followed by failure would be worse than half-effort and an excuse. They self-sabotage at the edge of an opportunity because some part of them does not believe they belong there.

**Mindset determines whether skill is applied or withheld.**

Conversely, people with developing skills but a strong mindset often progress faster than more capable colleagues, simply because they persist longer. They take the feedback — like Yvonne did. They try again. They treat each attempt as data rather than judgement.

When mindset and skill align, momentum becomes almost inevitable.

## Renewing the Inner Narrative

Mindset is not fixed.

It can be examined, challenged, and deliberately refined. Growth begins when you replace vague self-criticism with truthful self-assessment — not blind optimism, but honest, constructive thinking that acknowledges where you are while refusing to treat it as where you are permanently.

The language matters more than most people realise.

*"I'm not good at this" is a verdict.*

*"I'm still developing this" is a direction.*

One closes the door. The other leaves it open. And in professional life, keeping the door open — to growth, to improvement, to a version of yourself that is more capable than the current one — is one of the most strategic decisions you can make.

Language shapes belief. Belief shapes action.

## Clarity Checkpoint

*Identify one recurring limiting belief — a story you tell yourself that has quietly governed a decision, a hesitation, or a habit.*

Write it down plainly. Then write a truth-based alternative alongside it — not an affirmation, but an honest reframe that acknowledges growth rather than closing the door.

*For example:*

**Old story:** *"I'm not a confident speaker."*

**Honest reframe:** *"I haven't invested much in developing this yet. That is changeable."*

*Then ask: what is one action this week that the reframe makes possible, that the old story would have prevented?*

## Closing Reflection

Daniel and Yvonne received the same feedback.

One heard a criticism. The other heard a direction.

You cannot control every circumstance. You cannot guarantee every outcome. But you can influence the story you tell yourself about what is happening — and that story, repeated over months and years, shapes the professional you become.

Mindset does not guarantee success.

But it determines how far you are willing to go to find it.

Change your thinking,

**and new outcomes become possible.**

CHAPTER

# FOUR

## IDENTITY DRIVES BEHAVIOUR

Every January, James set goals.

Good ones. Specific, measurable, written down in the kind of notebook that felt like a commitment. He would spend an evening planning the year, and for the first few weeks everything moved in the right direction. He woke earlier. He exercised. He read before bed. He sent the email he had been putting off.

By February, most of it had quietly dissolved.

Not because James lacked discipline. Not because the goals were wrong. But because underneath every new behaviour was an older, more deeply held belief:

*I'm not really the kind of person who does these things.*

**He had changed his goals. He had not changed his identity.**

**Lasting change does not begin with goals.**

**It begins with identity.**

Many people try to modify behaviour without addressing who they believe they are. They set new targets, adopt new routines, and commit to new plans — and find themselves reverting to old patterns within weeks, sometimes days. This is not weakness. It is the predictable result of building new behaviours on an unchanged foundation.

Behaviour naturally follows identity.

**You do not act consistently against the person you believe yourself to be.**

## Why Behaviour Alone Rarely Lasts

Behaviour can be forced for a while.

Motivation carries most people through the first week. Some make it a month. But when pressure increases, results delay, or the novelty of change fades, behaviour that is not rooted in identity begins to weaken. The path of least resistance leads back to what feels natural — and what feels natural is almost always what is familiar.

You eventually return to what you are, not just what you intended.

Identity answers the deeper question behind every action: *"What kind of person am I?"* Until that question is honestly addressed, effort remains fragile — dependent on conditions being favourable and motivation being present, neither of which can be guaranteed.

## Identity as the Anchor for Consistency

Identity provides a different kind of stability — one that motivation cannot.

When you identify as someone who is disciplined, prepared, or intentional, actions begin to align naturally. You no longer rely on mood or momentum. You act in ways that feel congruent with who you understand yourself to be.

Consider the difference between these two statements:

> *"I am trying to read more."*

*"I am someone who learns continuously."*

The first is a goal. It depends on effort and reminder. The second is an identity. It generates behaviour because it is simply what that kind of person does.

**Identity makes consistency sustainable. Not through force, but through alignment.**

## The Cost of Misaligned Identity

Misalignment has a cost that rarely announces itself clearly.

It shows up as resistance — the low-grade friction you feel when you sit down to do something you know you should do but cannot seem to start. As procrastination on work that matters. As the quiet exhaustion of repeatedly committing to change and repeatedly falling short.

When your actions contradict your identity, the mind creates conflict. Tasks feel heavier than they should. Progress feels forced. Over time, discouragement sets in — not because the goal is wrong, but because the person pursuing it has not yet become someone for whom that goal is natural.

This explains a pattern many capable professionals recognise: intellectually committed to a change, genuinely wanting different results, but somehow unable to sustain the behaviour that would get them there.

**The problem is rarely will. It is alignment.**

## Identity Is Shaped Through Repetition

Identity is not something you declare once.

It is something you reinforce through repeated action.

Each action casts a vote for the type of person you are becoming. A single vote rarely decides anything. But over weeks and months, the accumulation of small, consistent choices builds something undeniable — evidence, visible to you and to others, of who you are.

This is why small actions carry more weight than their size suggests. They are not just tasks completed. They are identity reinforced.

Consistency is not just about outcomes.

**It is about becoming.**

## Choosing Identity Intentionally

Identity can be chosen.

Most people inherit their professional identity passively — shaped by early experiences, other people's expectations, the environments they happened to land in. They become a version of themselves that was never quite deliberately designed.

Choosing identity intentionally means deciding, with some deliberateness, what kind of professional you are becoming — and then acting in ways that make that true. Not waiting to feel ready. Not waiting for external validation. Acting in alignment with the identity now, even imperfectly, until the gap between who you are and who you are becoming begins to close.

**Growth accelerates when identity is chosen consciously rather than inherited passively.**

James's problem was not that he lacked goals. It was that he had never asked himself the more important question: who am I in the process of becoming? Until he could answer that honestly, every January would look the same.

## Clarity Checkpoint

*Complete this sentence without editing yourself:*

**"I am becoming the kind of person who __________."**

*Then ask yourself three honest questions:*

1. What is one small action this week that would cast a vote for that identity?
2. Where in my current behaviour is there clear misalignment with who I say I am becoming?
3. What is one habit or routine I have been forcing through willpower that alignment would make easier?

*Identity strengthens through action, not intention alone. Start with the smallest vote you can cast today.*

## Closing Reflection

Behaviour is visible. Identity is foundational.

When identity is clear, behaviour follows with less resistance and greater consistency. Not perfectly — consistency is never perfect. But sustainably, which matters far more.

If you want lasting change, do not start with what you want to do.

**Start with who you are becoming.**

Identity drives behaviour — and behaviour, sustained over time, shapes everything. The first four chapters of this book have been about how you think. *Clarity. Purpose. Mindset. Identity.* These are the internal foundations — the invisible architecture beneath every visible result.

But foundations are only as powerful as what is built on them.

The next section asks a different question: not how you think, but how you *show up*. Day after day. In ordinary circumstances. Without applause.

**That is where consistency lives.**

SECTION II

# CONSISTENCY

*How You Show Up*

CHAPTER
# FIVE
# CONSISTENCY: THE UNCELEBRATED ADVANTAGE

## Nobody noticed when Rachel started.

She did not announce it. There was no moment of visible commitment, no declaration to her manager or her team. She simply decided, one quiet Monday morning, to spend thirty minutes before her first meeting reading about her industry. Not every day. Just most days.

For the first few months, nothing visible changed.

Then, gradually, things did. She started asking sharper questions in meetings. She connected trends her colleagues had not yet noticed. She began contributing ideas that felt ahead of the room. Within a year, her manager had started describing her as one of the most "strategically minded" people on the team.

When a colleague asked what had changed, Rachel struggled to point to anything specific.

Nothing had changed dramatically.

**Everything had changed consistently.**

**Consistency rarely draws attention.**

It does not announce itself with breakthroughs or dramatic turns. Most days, it looks ordinary — even unimpressive. The same effort. The same routine. The same discipline applied quietly, in circumstances where no one is watching and no applause is coming.

And yet, consistency is one of the most reliable forces behind meaningful professional progress.

What many people admire as talent or luck is often the outcome of steady, repeated effort over time — effort that was invisible while it was accumulating and only became visible once it had compounded into something undeniable.

## Why Consistency Is Undervalued

Modern work culture celebrates intensity.

We praise the late nights, the sprint, the all-in launch. We admire bursts of productivity and the visible momentum of someone moving fast. Consistency, by contrast, feels slow. It lacks drama. It does not make a good story — at least not while it is happening.

But intensity fades.

**Consistency endures.**

Intensity relies on motivation — and motivation is unreliable. It peaks, dips, and disappears entirely in the face of frustration, fatigue, or a long stretch without visible reward. Consistency relies on something sturdier: commitment. A decision made in advance that is not renegotiated every morning based on mood.

That is the quiet power of consistency. It shows up not because the conditions are right, but because the decision has already been made.

## Consistency Builds Trust With Yourself

One of the most overlooked benefits of consistency has nothing to do with other people.

**It is self-trust.**

Every time you follow through on a commitment you made to yourself — however small — you send a message to your own mind: *I can be counted on.* Repeated often enough, that message becomes a belief. And that belief becomes the foundation of genuine, durable confidence.

Inconsistency runs this process in reverse.

When you repeatedly commit and fail to follow through — even on small things, even with good reason — you erode internal credibility. Not dramatically. But quietly, over time, you begin to discount your own intentions. You stop fully believing yourself when you set a goal, because experience has taught you that your follow-through is uncertain.

This is why starting small matters so much. It is not just about lowering the barrier to action. It is about accumulating evidence of reliability — evidence that you are someone who does what they say they will do.

**Consistency repairs self-trust one kept promise at a time.**

## Consistency Reduces Mental Resistance

When actions are inconsistent, every task requires negotiation.

> *Should I do this today? Can it wait until tomorrow? Am I in the right mindset for this right now?*

These questions seem small but they are expensive. Each one spends a little mental energy, narrows focus, and opens the door to avoidance. Over the course of a day, the cumulative cost of constant self-negotiation is significant — energy spent on deciding rather than doing.

Consistency removes those questions entirely.

When a behaviour is consistent, the decision has already been made. Structure replaces debate. The energy that would have been spent on persuading yourself is preserved for the actual work. Over time, this compounds — consistent people are not working harder than inconsistent ones. They are working with less friction.

## Consistency Makes Progress Inevitable

Results do not follow occasional effort.

They follow what is repeated.

What you do sporadically may impress.

**What you do consistently produces outcomes.**

Consistency does not guarantee speed. Some progress is slow regardless of how reliably you show up. But it guarantees direction — a steady movement toward something, even when any given day feels like standing still.

This is the quiet logic of compounding. Small, consistent inputs produce results that eventually exceed what occasional bursts of effort ever could. Not because any single day was exceptional, but because none of them were wasted.

## The Role of Small Actions

Consistency does not require grand gestures.

In fact, grand gestures are often the enemy of consistency. They raise the stakes of showing up. They make it harder to begin on days when energy is low or conditions are imperfect. They attach performance to an act that simply needs to happen.

Small actions, by contrast, lower the cost of entry. They are easy to start. They are harder to justify skipping. And over time, they accumulate into results that look, to outside observers, like talent or exceptional discipline

— when in reality they are the product of something simpler and more available: just showing up, quietly and reliably, more days than not.

Rachel's thirty minutes did not look like much on any individual morning.

**Across a year, it was a significant professional investment.**

## Clarity Checkpoint

*Choose one behaviour that supports the person you are becoming.*

Make it small enough that you cannot justify skipping it on a difficult day. Then answer these questions:

1. When, specifically, will this happen each day or week?
2. What is the smallest version of this that still counts?
3. Where in your recent behaviour has inconsistency cost you self-trust?

*Consistency is built on uneventful days, not exceptional ones. Commit to showing up on the ordinary ones first.*

## Closing Reflection

Nobody noticed when Rachel started.

**That is exactly how consistency works.**

It does not ask for recognition while it is building. It does not require an audience to function. It simply accumulates — quietly, reliably — until one day the results become visible and people wonder how it happened.

Those who understand its power stop chasing intensity and begin building rhythm. They trade the satisfaction of urgency for the deeper satisfaction of reliability. And over time, they discover that quiet effort, faithfully applied, produces results that brilliant bursts of energy rarely can.

Consistency is not exciting.

But it is effective.

**And that is why it remains the most underrated advantage available to anyone willing to simply show up.**

CHAPTER

# SIX

# DISCIPLINE IS SELF-RESPECT

For most of his career, Kevin thought of discipline as something imposed on him.

Deadlines were imposed. Targets were imposed. The expectation that he would be prepared, responsive, and reliable — all of it felt like external pressure, a weight he carried because the job required it. Discipline, in his mind, was the mechanism by which the organisation extracted performance from people who might otherwise coast.

He was disciplined, by most measures. But it cost him something every day. There was always a low-level resistance to it — a sense of being managed, contained, pressed into shape.

The shift came not through a new system or a management course, but through a single reframing question a mentor asked him:

> *"When you follow through on something, Kevin — who are you doing that for?"*

He had never considered that the answer might be himself.

**Discipline is often misunderstood.**

Many professionals associate it with restriction, severity, and pressure — a force required to control behaviour or compensate for weakness. It is experienced as something done to them rather than something chosen by them. And when discipline feels like control, it feels like resistance.

But discipline, at its core, is not punishment.

**It is self-respect in action.**

Discipline is the decision to honour your commitments to yourself, even when no one is watching. It reflects how seriously you take your own intentions — not what others expect of you, but what you have decided matters to you.

## Why Discipline Is Not About Force

Force relies on pressure.

And pressure eventually fails.

Discipline sustained through external expectation alone is fragile. It holds as long as someone is watching, as long as the consequences of falling short are visible. Remove the pressure, and the behaviour collapses — not because the person is weak, but because the behaviour was never truly theirs.

Real discipline relies on clarity and choice. It is not about pushing harder — it is about deciding more clearly.

When you are disciplined in this sense, you are not fighting yourself. You are aligned with what you value. Actions follow intention not because they are enforced from outside, but because they make sense from within.

Discipline feels lighter when it is rooted in purpose. Not effortless — but lighter. There is a difference between the weight of something you are forced to carry and the weight of something you have chosen to build.

## Self-Respect Shapes Behaviour

People naturally protect what they value.

This is not a motivational principle. It is simply how human beings operate.

When you respect your time, you protect it from commitments that do not deserve it. When you respect your energy, you become more deliberate about where it goes. When you respect your direction, you stop tolerating behaviour in yourself that contradicts it.

**Discipline is the visible expression of that respect.**

This reframe matters because it locates the source of discipline in the right place. A lack of discipline is rarely a motivation problem. More often, it reflects a gap between what a person says they value and what their daily behaviour reveals they actually prioritise.

Close that gap — not by trying harder, but by taking yourself more seriously — and discipline begins to feel less like a burden and more like an expression of who you are.

## Discipline Builds Inner Trust

In Chapter 5, we saw how consistency builds self-trust through repeated action.

Discipline is that principle applied with intention.

Each disciplined action reinforces internal credibility — the quiet accumulation of evidence that you are someone who follows through. Not for recognition. Not under observation. But because you said you would, and that matters to you.

Over time, this internal trust becomes something more durable than motivation. Motivation is conditional — it depends on how you feel, on how the week is going, on whether the work feels rewarding right now.

Self-trust is unconditional. It shows up on difficult days precisely because it is not dependent on conditions being favourable.

Confidence does not come from words spoken aloud.

**It comes from promises kept quietly.**

## Discipline Creates Freedom

At first glance, discipline can feel like the opposite of freedom.

Rules, routines, commitments — these feel like constraints. And they are. But they are constraints you have chosen, which makes them structurally different from the constraints imposed by chaos, reactive decision-making, and the accumulated consequences of not following through.

Consider what an undisciplined week actually looks like. Decisions that have to be made under pressure because they were avoided when there was time. Energy spent managing the fallout of commitments not honoured. Mental space occupied by the low-grade anxiety of things left unfinished. Opportunities missed not from lack of ability, but from lack of readiness.

**That is not freedom. That is the most constrained way to work.**

Discipline, by contrast, removes constant negotiation. It simplifies decision-making, reduces emotional friction, and replaces reactive chaos with intentional structure. The person who has decided in advance how they will use their mornings, which commitments they will honour, and what they will say no to — that person operates with a kind of daily freedom that the undisciplined person rarely experiences.

Discipline narrows choices so that progress can widen.

## Discipline Thrives in Structure

Discipline is not sustained by willpower alone.

Willpower is a depleting resource. It is strongest in the morning, weakens through the day, and is most unreliable precisely when it is most needed — when you are tired, pressured, or facing something difficult.

Discipline thrives in structure — in routines, boundaries, and environments designed to make the right behaviour easier and the wrong behaviour harder. When discipline is embedded into daily systems, it no longer depends on summoning effort from scratch each time. The structure does much of the work.

There is a principle that captures this precisely:

> *You do not rise to the level of your intentions.*
>
> ***You fall to the level of your structure.***

Build structures that support who you are becoming, and discipline becomes less about force and more about design.

## Clarity Checkpoint

*Think of discipline not as self-control, but as self-respect. Then answer honestly:*

1. Where in your current behaviour is there a clear gap between what you say you value and what your daily actions reveal?
2. Which commitment to yourself have you been negotiating around rather than simply honouring?
3. What is one structure — a routine, boundary, or environment change — that would make the right behaviour easier without relying on willpower?

*Discipline grows through consistency, not intensity. Choose one commitment. Honour it without negotiation. Then do it again.*

## Closing Reflection

Kevin eventually found a different relationship with discipline.

Not by working harder or holding himself to stricter standards, but by shifting the question from *"What do they expect of me?"* to *"What do I expect of myself?"* The resistance did not disappear overnight. But it began to soften, because discipline was no longer something happening to him. It was something he was choosing.

Discipline is not about denying yourself.

**It is about honouring yourself.**

It reflects how much you value your time, your potential, and your direction. When discipline becomes an act of self-respect rather than self-control, it stops feeling heavy — and starts feeling like the most natural expression of who you are choosing to become.

**Respect yourself enough to follow through.**

CHAPTER

# SEVEN

## SMALL WINS BUILD CONFIDENCE

Nina had been meaning to apply for the role for three weeks.

She had read the job description carefully. She had quietly told herself she wanted it. She had even opened a blank document and typed her name at the top of the application.

Then she had closed it.

Not because she was unqualified. Her manager had told her directly that she was ready. Not because the timing was wrong. The window was open for another two weeks. But because every time she sat down to begin, the same thought arrived:

*"I'll do it when I feel more confident."*

The deadline passed. The role was filled. Nina remained exactly where she had been, waiting for a feeling that was never going to arrive the way she imagined it would.

Because confidence does not come before the action.

**It comes from it.**

**Confidence is often treated as a personality trait.**

Some people are described as naturally confident, others as inherently unsure. The implication is that confidence is fixed — either present or absent, something you have or you lack.

But confidence is rarely something you are born with.

**It is something you build.**

Confidence grows from evidence — internal evidence, accumulated through action, that you are someone capable of doing what you say you will do. And the most reliable source of that evidence is not a single breakthrough moment, but small wins repeated consistently over time.

## Why Confidence Rarely Arrives First

Many people operate on an assumption that keeps them permanently stuck:

> *Confidence must come before action.*

They wait to feel ready. They wait for certainty, for clarity, for the internal green light that tells them the moment is right. When the feeling does not arrive, the action is postponed. And when the action is postponed, the confidence never arrives either — because confidence is built through action, not through waiting.

This is not a character flaw. It is a misunderstanding of sequence.

Small actions completed fully send a clear signal to the mind: *I can do what I say I will do.* That signal, repeated consistently, becomes the foundation of genuine confidence. Not a feeling that arrives before the work, but a belief earned through it.

## Small Wins Create Momentum

Momentum does not require dramatic breakthroughs.

It requires movement.

Each completed task, no matter how small, reduces resistance to the next one. It lowers the psychological cost of beginning. It demonstrates — to yourself, quietly — that you are someone who starts things and finishes them. Over time, that demonstration becomes a kind of forward pull.

**Motivation follows motion, not the other way around.**

This is why starting — even imperfectly, even with a version of the work that you know needs refinement — is almost always more valuable than waiting for the conditions to be right. The act of beginning creates conditions that waiting cannot.

## Small Wins Shrink Fear

Fear thrives in inaction.

When tasks sit unfinished, when decisions are deferred, when action is perpetually postponed — the space that opens up is filled not with rest but with doubt. Uncertainty expands. The task grows in imagination until it occupies far more mental space than the actual work would require.

**Action shrinks fear — not by eliminating it, but by replacing speculation with experience.**

When you complete a small task you have been avoiding, you discover something important: it was rarely as difficult as the avoidance made it feel. The gap between the feared version of a thing and the actual experience of doing it is almost always narrower than anticipated. Small wins, repeated regularly, teach you to trust that gap.

## Why Small Wins Matter More Than Big Goals

Big goals have a complicated relationship with confidence.

They inspire, which is valuable. But they also make the distance visible in a way that can be paralyzing. When a goal is large and distant, every day that passes without visible progress can feel like failure — even when steady, necessary groundwork is being laid.

Small wins solve this problem.

They break distance into steps. They make progress visible on a timescale that sustains effort. They provide daily evidence that growth is happening — not eventually, but now. And crucially, they keep the confidence loop running: action produces evidence, evidence builds belief, belief sustains action.

The professional who strings together consistent small wins often outpaces the one who is saving their effort for a single defining moment — because the defining moment, when it arrives, is met with readiness that only accumulated action can build.

## The Perfection Trap

Perfectionism looks like high standards.

**Often, it is fear with a more respectable name.**

Waiting until the work is perfect before sharing it. Holding back from applying until every qualification is solidly met. Avoiding the conversation until the exact right words are ready. These behaviours feel like quality control. In practice, they are a way of avoiding the vulnerability of being seen trying — and possibly falling short.

But perfection is not where confidence lives. Completion is.

Every finished draft, every submitted application, every conversation started despite uncertainty — these are the raw materials of confidence. Not because they are flawless, but because they happened. They produced evidence. They moved something forward.

Progress favours those willing to finish imperfectly and improve over time.

## Clarity Checkpoint

*Identify one action you have been postponing while waiting to feel ready or confident enough.*

Then answer honestly:

1. Is this actually a readiness problem — or a confidence problem disguised as one?
2. What is the smallest version of this action I could complete today — not perfectly, but fully?
3. Where in my recent work have I let perfection become a reason for inaction?

*Confidence is not something you wait for. It is something you earn — one completed action at a time. Start today.*

## Closing Reflection

The deadline passed for Nina.

**But the lesson did not.**

When the next opportunity arrived, she did not wait to feel ready. She started the application the same day she read the brief. It was imperfect. She submitted it anyway. She did not get that role either, but she got the one after it — and she got it in part because by then she had built the evidence, through repeated small actions, that she was someone who showed up.

Confidence is not something you wait for.

**It is something you earn.**

Build the habit of finishing small things well. Acknowledge the completion. Let the evidence accumulate. Confidence will follow — not as a feeling that precedes the work, but as a truth earned through it.

The three chapters of Section II have been about how you show up. *Consistency. Discipline. Small wins.* These are the daily practices that turn the internal foundations of Section I into visible, reliable behaviour.

But showing up consistently is only part of the picture.

The next section asks what you are building while you show up. Not just whether you are present — but whether you are *growing.* Learning, developing courage, preparing for what is coming, and making your contribution visible.

**That is where capability lives.**

SECTION III

# CAPABILITY

*How You Grow*

CHAPTER

# EIGHT

## LEARNING IS A CAREER ADVANTAGE

For twelve years, Thomas had been one of the most capable people in the room.

He had built his reputation steadily — through reliability, deep expertise, and a consistency that others leaned on. When problems arose in his area, people came to Thomas. When new team members needed orienting, Thomas was the reference point. He was, in the truest sense, indispensable.

Then the industry shifted.

Not dramatically — there was no single disruption, no overnight transformation. Just a gradual change in tools, methods, and expectations over three or four years. Thomas noticed it. He simply assumed his experience would carry him through it.

By the time he recognised the gap, it had become wide enough that closing it required real effort — not the easy, incremental learning of someone who had stayed current, but the harder work of catching up while the field kept moving.

Thomas had not become less capable. He had simply stopped growing at the moment his career most needed him to continue.

The greatest career risk is rarely a lack of talent.

**It is the decision — often gradual, often unconscious — to stop learning.**

**The world of work does not stand still.**

Roles evolve. Tools change. Expectations rise. What made someone exceptional five years ago may make them merely competent today, and insufficient tomorrow. In this environment, learning is no longer something you do early in your career and then move past.

It has become a posture — a way of engaging with change without fear.

Those who continue learning remain relevant. Those who stop gradually lose their edge — not suddenly, but steadily, in ways that become visible only once the gap has already grown.

## Why Learning Protects Relevance

Many professionals become competent and then comfortable.

Competence is earned and should be valued. But comfort, left unchecked, becomes the enemy of continued growth. When experience feels sufficient, learning feels optional. And when learning feels optional, it is the first thing quietly dropped when days get busy.

The professional who relies entirely on past experience is drawing down an account without making deposits. For a while, the balance holds. But as the environment shifts — as it always does — the gap between what is known and what is now required begins to widen.

**Learning closes that gap before it becomes costly.**

It allows you to adapt without panic and respond without defensiveness — not by chasing every trend, but by staying genuinely curious about what matters most in your field and what is beginning to change.

**Relevance is sustained, not assumed.**

## Learning Signals Readiness

Curiosity is visible.

The person who asks a question that reveals they have been thinking beyond the immediate task. The one who references something they read that connects to the problem being discussed. The colleague who takes on a new responsibility not because they were asked, but because they had been quietly preparing.

These moments are noticed — not always explicitly, but consistently.

When you learn proactively, you signal something that cannot be manufactured: genuine openness, intellectual humility, and forward motion. You demonstrate that you are preparing for what is next, not clinging to what is familiar. Leaders notice this — not because they are looking for it specifically, but because its absence is equally visible.

Opportunity often follows those who are already growing because such people reduce the risk of the investment. Promoting someone who is actively learning is a safer bet than promoting someone who peaked five years ago and has been coasting since.

**Learning communicates readiness long before promotion or recognition arrives.**

## Learning Builds Confidence in Change

Change is unsettling when you feel unprepared.

The professional who has not been learning approaches change defensively. New tools feel threatening. Shifting expectations feel like criticism. Organisational transformation feels like displacement. The instinct is to protect what was built rather than engage with what is coming.

Learning changes that orientation entirely.

It replaces fear with familiarity and confusion with context. Even when you do not have all the answers, regular learning builds the confidence to engage with new challenges thoughtfully rather than fearfully. You know you are not standing still, which means change feels less like a threat and more like an extension of what you have already been doing.

Learning does not remove complexity.

**It equips you to navigate it.**

## Learning Is Not About Accumulation

There is a version of learning that looks productive but produces very little.

It is the collection of information — articles saved but never applied, courses started but never finished, books read quickly and never revisited. It creates the feeling of learning without the substance. The shelf looks impressive. The practice remains unchanged.

**Effective learning is different. It is selective, applied, and directional.**

It asks not "what is interesting?" but "what do I need to understand in order to do this better?" It focuses on depth over volume, on application over awareness. Not everything needs to be mastered. What matters is learning what genuinely supports your direction — and then using it.

Depth matters more than volume.

**Learning becomes powerful when it is intentional.**

## Learning as a Long-Term Strategy

Careers are marathons, not sprints.

And like any marathon, the risk is not always visible at the start. Early career, most professionals are naturally in learning mode — everything is new, adaptation is constant, and growth is almost unavoidable. The risk arrives later, when competence has been established and the pressure to keep learning feels less urgent.

**This is the moment that most determines the shape of a career.**

Those who treat learning as an ongoing strategy — not an early-career necessity but a lifelong professional practice — tend to experience multiple seasons of relevance and contribution rather than a single peak followed by a long decline. They remain elastic: able to stretch into new roles, new responsibilities, and new contexts without the brittleness that comes from too long a period without growth.

Learning keeps a career elastic.

Thomas's story did not end badly — he caught up, eventually, through deliberate effort and some humility. But he lost years of compounding advantage he could have retained simply by maintaining the learning habit at the moment he felt least like he needed it.

## Clarity Checkpoint

*Identify one area of your work that is changing — a skill shifting, a tool evolving, an expectation rising.*

Then answer honestly:

1. Am I currently learning about this area — or assuming my existing knowledge is sufficient?
2. What is the gap between what I currently know and what this role or field now requires?
3. What is one specific, applied learning I could commit to this week — not to collect information, but to change how I work?

*Fifteen minutes of focused, applied learning — done consistently — compounds significantly over a year. Learning does not require urgency. It requires continuity.*

## Closing Reflection

Thomas was not undone by a lack of talent or effort.

**He was undone by a quiet assumption that competence, once achieved, was sufficient.**

The future of work will continue to change — faster, in all likelihood, than most of us anticipate. Those who remain curious will remain capable. Those who keep learning will keep growing. Not because they are chasing every new development, but because they have decided that growth is not a phase they passed through but a practice they maintain.

Learning is not a distraction from your career.

**It is one of its greatest and most enduring advantages.**

CHAPTER

# NINE

## COURAGE PRECEDES GROWTH

Nobody in the room knew that Sofia was terrified.

She had been asked to present her project findings to the senior leadership team — twelve people around a table, each of them two or three levels above her. She had prepared thoroughly. She knew the material. But as she stood up to begin, the familiar voice arrived:

*"You are not ready for this room."*

She presented anyway.

It was not perfect. She spoke faster than she intended in the first few minutes. One question from the CFO caught her off balance. But she answered it honestly, said clearly what she did not yet know, and finished with a recommendation that the team later acted on.

Afterwards, her director told her it was one of the most credible presentations he had seen from someone at her level.

Sofia had not felt ready.

**She had simply decided that not feeling ready was not a reason to stop.**

**Growth is often described as exciting.**

In reality, growth is usually uncomfortable first.

Before clarity comes uncertainty. Before confidence comes hesitation. Before progress comes courage.

Most meaningful growth begins not with certainty, but with a decision to move despite incomplete information. Courage is the bridge between learning and application — the force that closes the gap between what you know and what you are willing to do with it.

## Why Growth Rarely Feels Safe

Many people delay growth because they wait for reassurance.

They want confidence before action, certainty before commitment, and guarantees before risk. These desires are entirely understandable. But growth rarely offers these conditions in advance — because growth, by definition, takes you beyond what you already know how to do.

If you already felt capable and safe, it would not be growth.

Growth asks for movement without full visibility. It requires stepping into circumstances where the outcome is genuinely uncertain — where things might not go well, where you might fall short, where the gap between who you are now and who the situation requires might become temporarily visible to others.

Courage does not eliminate that fear.

**It acknowledges it and moves anyway.**

## Courage Begins Internally

Courage is often imagined as a public act.

We picture it as something visible and dramatic — the bold declaration, the stand taken in front of an audience, the risk taken in a moment everyone remembers. But most professional courage looks nothing like that.

**Most of it is private.**

It is the quiet decision to apply for a role when you feel underqualified. To contribute a perspective in a meeting where more senior voices dominate. To start the project you have been putting off because you are not yet sure it will succeed. To have the honest conversation you have been avoiding because the relationship feels too important to risk.

No one applauds these moments. They rarely appear in performance reviews or career retrospectives. But they shape trajectories in ways that are disproportionate to their size, because every private act of courage expands the boundary of what feels possible.

Sofia's courage was not in the performance.

**It was in the decision, made alone before anyone could see it, to stand up anyway.**

## Courage Reveals Capacity

Many people underestimate themselves because they have never tested their limits.

This is not modesty. It is simply the result of staying within boundaries that feel safe. Inside those boundaries, ability remains theoretical — plausible but unconfirmed. It is only when you act, often despite doubt, that you discover what you are actually capable of.

**Action reveals what hesitation hides.**

When you act courageously — when you take on the assignment that stretches you, have the conversation you have been avoiding, or step into a room where you feel out of place — you produce evidence about your own capability that no amount of preparation or reflection could generate. Capacity expands through experience, not contemplation.

This is why courage and learning are inseparable. In Chapter 8, we saw that effective learning requires application, not just accumulation.

Courage is what makes application possible — it is the willingness to use what you have learned in conditions where it might not be enough yet.

**Growth often arrives disguised as discomfort.**

## The Cost of Avoided Courage

Avoidance feels protective.

It preserves the status quo. It keeps the relationship intact, the reputation unrisked, the possibility of failure safely theoretical. In the short term, avoidance is almost always the more comfortable choice.

**But it is expensive.**

Opportunities pass while you are waiting to feel ready. Skills stagnate because the situations that develop them are avoided. Confidence erodes — not from failure, but from the accumulation of moments where you chose not to try. And over time, something more corrosive than fear begins to settle in.

**Regret.**

Regret is harder to carry than the discomfort of trying and falling short. Fear at least keeps company with possibility. Regret arrives after the door has closed — after the role was filled, the window passed, the season moved on without you.

Courage may feel costly in the moment.

**Avoidance costs more in the long run.**

## Courage Is a Practice, Not a Trait

Courage is not a fixed quantity — something you either possess or lack.

It is a capacity that grows through use. Each courageous act — however small, however private — reduces resistance to the next one. The boundary of what feels manageable shifts outward. Over time, situations that once felt genuinely intimidating begin to feel merely challenging, and then simply familiar.

You do not become courageous by waiting.

**You become courageous by acting.**

The professional who takes one small courageous step this week is slightly more capable of taking a larger one next month. The person who avoids difficult action this week makes avoidance slightly more automatic next time. Small acts of courage, like small wins, compound in directions you cannot fully see until you are further along.

## Clarity Checkpoint

*Identify one area where fear or discomfort has been delaying action.*

Then answer honestly:

1. Is this a genuine readiness gap — or avoidance wearing the clothes of caution?
2. What is the smallest courageous step I could take this week — one that moves toward the discomfort rather than away from it?
3. If I continue avoiding this for another year, what will I most likely regret?

*Courage often begins small. The goal is not to eliminate the discomfort — it is to move despite it.*

## Closing Reflection

Sofia's presentation was not flawless.

But it was real. It was honest. And it moved her forward in ways that waiting for a perfect moment never could have.

Growth does not wait for perfect conditions.

**It responds to courage.**

When you move despite uncertainty, learning turns into capability and potential turns into progress. The discomfort does not disappear — but your relationship with it changes. What once felt like a reason to stop becomes simply part of what growth feels like.

Courage may not guarantee success.

**But it always moves you forward.**

## CHAPTER
# TEN
# PREPARATION CREATES CONFIDENCE

### Two people walked into the same meeting.

Both had been invited to present on the same topic. Both had the same amount of time to prepare. Both were capable, experienced, and respected within the organisation.

The first, Andre, had spent the days before the meeting in the material — reviewing the data, anticipating the questions most likely to arise, thinking through the implications of each finding, and stress-testing his recommendation against the objections he expected. He was not certain everything would go smoothly. But he was ready.

The second had been busy. The preparation had been left until the morning of the meeting, assembled quickly from notes and memory. The material was familiar. The depth was not.

When the first difficult question arrived, Andre paused, considered it, and answered with the measured confidence of someone who had already thought this through. His counterpart hesitated, qualified, backtracked slightly — not because they lacked the knowledge, but because they had not had time to organise it.

Afterwards, the room's perception of the two was strikingly different.

Not because of ability.

**Because of readiness.**

**Confidence is often mistaken for charisma.**

Some people appear naturally assured — comfortable speaking, decisive under pressure, quick to respond. It is easy to assume that confidence is a quality they were born with or somehow acquired through personality rather than practice.

**More often, it is built quietly through preparation.**

Prepared people move differently. They listen carefully because they are not anxious about what comes next. They respond thoughtfully because they have already considered the terrain. They act without panic because the work was done before the moment arrived.

Not because they know everything.

**Because they are ready.**

## Why Confidence Fades Without Preparation

When preparation is absent, pressure feels heavier than it needs to.

Decisions become rushed because there is no prior thinking to draw on. Mistakes feel costly because there is no preparation buffer to absorb them. Uncertainty breeds anxiety because familiarity — the thing that calms the nervous system in high-stakes moments — is missing.

This is the crucial distinction the original offers: unprepared people doubt themselves not because they lack ability, but because they lack readiness.

**That distinction matters.**

Ability is slow to build and difficult to demonstrate in the moment. Readiness can be created in advance, deliberately, for any specific situation you can anticipate. A person who is less naturally gifted but thoroughly prepared will almost always outperform someone more talented but underprepared — because talent without readiness is potential, not performance.

## Preparation Reduces Anxiety

Anxiety thrives in uncertainty.

The mind in an unprepared state is essentially improvising — reacting to each moment without the foundation of prior thought. That improvisation feels like pressure. And pressure, sustained without release, becomes anxiety.

Preparation replaces guessing with familiarity. It does not eliminate risk or guarantee a smooth outcome. But it reduces surprise — and reducing surprise is one of the most reliable ways to reduce anxiety. When you have already thought through the likely challenges, they arrive as expected rather than as shocks.

**Calm under pressure is often the visible sign of invisible work done in advance.**

When others see someone handle a difficult moment with composure, they tend to attribute it to temperament or natural confidence. In most cases, it is preparation. The composure was earned before the room, not in it.

## Preparation Accelerates Opportunity

Opportunity rarely announces itself with advance notice.

It appears in a conversation that turns unexpectedly significant. In a question asked of the room that you happen to be ready to answer. In a gap that opens when someone else cannot deliver and you can. In a moment when a decision-maker needs someone they can trust to step up quickly.

Prepared people are positioned for these moments because they are not scrambling to get ready when the moment arrives. They are already there.

This is the quiet advantage of ongoing preparation: it shortens the distance between opportunity and action to almost nothing. You do not need time to prepare — you have already prepared. The moment becomes available in a way it simply is not for the person who would need days to get ready.

**Luck, in professional life, has a strong correlation with preparation.**

## Preparation Builds Credibility

Preparation communicates something that cannot be faked in the moment.

It communicates seriousness — the signal that you took this, and the people involved, seriously enough to do the work before arriving. People notice this, often without being able to articulate precisely what they are noticing. They feel the difference between someone who came prepared and someone who did not.

Over time, consistent preparation builds something more durable than a good impression in any single meeting. It builds a reputation — the reliable expectation in others' minds that engaging with you will be worthwhile, that your contributions will be considered, that you can be trusted to show up ready.

**Trust is earned quietly, through readiness.**

This connects directly to Chapter 9's Sofia. Her courage in the presentation room landed well partly because she had prepared thoroughly. The courage was what made her step up. The preparation was what made the step credible.

## Preparation Creates Optionality

There is a concept that captures one of preparation's most underappreciated benefits: optionality.

Optionality means having choices available that others do not — not because you are more talented, but because you are more ready. The professional who has kept their skills current, their thinking sharp, and their professional presence maintained has more options in any given situation than the one who has let these things drift.

They can say yes to things others cannot. They can move quickly when others need time. They can pivot without panic when circumstances change, because the preparation that matters is already done.

Preparation is not a one-time effort.

It is a habit — built through consistent learning, regular reflection, and the deliberate maintenance of the professional assets that will matter when the next opportunity arrives. Those who prepare regularly are never starting from scratch. They are always building on a foundation that is already in place.

**Preparation compounds.**

## Clarity Checkpoint

*Choose one professional asset that matters to where you are heading.*

It might be your ability to present, your depth in a particular subject area, your communication style, your professional network, or your awareness of how your field is changing. Then answer honestly:

1. How prepared am I, right now, for the next significant opportunity in my field?
2. Where is there a preparation gap that, if closed, would meaningfully change what I can say yes to?
3. What is one specific improvement to this asset I could make this week — not urgently, but consistently?

*Confidence is not bravado. It is readiness made visible. Prepare well — then move calmly when the moment arrives.*

## Closing Reflection

Andre and his colleague had the same ability.

**The room experienced them as very different people.**

That gap — between what you are capable of and what others experience you as capable of — is often a preparation gap. Not a talent gap, not a confidence gap, not a personality gap.

A readiness gap.

Confidence is not bravado.

**It is readiness made visible.**

When preparation becomes a habit rather than a last-minute effort, confidence becomes steady rather than fragile — available not just when conditions are favourable but in every room, at every level, whenever the moment arrives.

Prepare well.

**Then move calmly when the moment arrives.**

CHAPTER

# ELEVEN

## VALUE SPEAKS LOUDER THAN TITLES

Elena had the title.

Senior Manager. Five years in the role. A team of eight reporting to her, a budget she controlled, and a seat at the table in meetings where decisions were made. By every formal measure, she held real authority.

Yet when the organisation needed someone to lead the most visible project of the year, the assignment went to David — two levels below Elena, no direct reports, no budget of his own.

Elena was frustrated. She felt bypassed.

But the people making the decision had watched David for two years. They had watched him notice problems before they were assigned to anyone. They had seen him find solutions quietly, without announcement. They had experienced the quality of his thinking in rooms where he had no formal standing at all. When it came time to choose someone they trusted with something important, his name came up without debate.

Elena had the title.

**David had the value.**

**Titles still matter.**

But they matter less than they used to.

In today's workplace, credibility is no longer sustained by position alone. Roles may open doors, but value is what keeps them open. The marketplace increasingly rewards those who make things better — not those who simply hold a role.

A title can introduce you.

**Value is what makes people remember you.**

## The Shift From Position to Contribution

For most of the twentieth century, professional authority flowed primarily from hierarchy.

If you held the title, influence followed. If you stayed long enough in the right organisation, credibility accumulated through tenure. The system was relatively predictable: rise through the levels, accumulate status, and the authority to be heard would come with the position.

That model has changed significantly.

Today, influence is increasingly earned through contribution rather than conferred through position. Organisations move faster, structures flatten, and the people who attract attention and trust are those who solve real problems — regardless of where they sit on the org chart.

This shift creates both a risk and an opportunity.

The risk: professionals who rely on title rather than contribution become progressively less influential as the title does less of the work. The opportunity: those without seniority can build genuine influence through the quality and consistency of what they contribute.

**Value travels faster than titles.**

## Speaking in Outcomes, Not Tasks

One of the most practical ways to communicate value is to change the language you use to describe your work.

**Tasks describe what you do. Outcomes explain why it matters.**

Many capable professionals consistently undersell themselves by defaulting to task language. In performance conversations, interviews, and even everyday interactions, they describe responsibilities rather than results. They say what they handle, not what changes because they handle it well.

The distinction matters more than most people realise. Consider the difference between:

> *"I manage the client reporting process."*
>
> *"I reduced client reporting time by 40% and improved accuracy, which freed the team to focus on higher-value work."*

Both describe the same person doing the same work. One communicates a task. The other communicates value. When you speak in outcomes, your work becomes visible in a way that task descriptions never achieve.

## Making Impact Measurable

Value becomes undeniable when it can be seen.

This does not require elaborate metrics or a background in data analysis. It requires only the discipline to ask one honest question about your work:

> ***What changed because I was involved?***

Where did efficiency improve? Where did quality rise? Where did time reduce, clarity increase, or risk diminish? Where did a team perform better, a client stay longer, or a decision get made faster?

These questions do not require a spreadsheet. They require honest reflection and the willingness to name the difference your work makes —

to yourself first, and then to the people whose trust and decisions shape your career.

**Numbers turn contribution into evidence. Evidence turns contribution into credibility.**

## Becoming a Problem Solver

Anyone can complete assigned work.

It is the baseline expectation of employment. Completing what you are asked to do is necessary — but it is not what builds a reputation. What builds a reputation is what you do beyond the assignment.

**Value grows when you solve unassigned problems.**

This means noticing the gap no one has named yet. Anticipating the need before it becomes urgent. Offering a solution before being asked for one. These behaviours signal something that titles cannot convey: genuine investment in the outcome, not just the task.

David's value was built this way — not through a single impressive moment, but through a consistent pattern of noticing, thinking, and contributing that accumulated over two years into an unspoken reputation. When the organisation needed someone to trust with something important, that reputation did the speaking.

**Problem solvers do not wait to be given authority. They earn it through demonstrated judgement.**

## Value Builds Influence Quietly

Influence built through value does not announce itself.

It accumulates in the background, through experiences others have of your work. The colleague who remembers the time you caught the error before it became a problem. The manager who recalls the meeting where your question changed the direction of the discussion. The client who tells someone else that you are the person they trust to get things right.

None of those moments felt like influence-building at the time. They were simply good work, done well, consistently. But over time, the accumulation of those experiences in the minds of the people around you becomes something durable — a reputation that opens doors, earns trust, and creates opportunities that titles alone never could.

**Value speaks long after introductions are forgotten.**

## Clarity Checkpoint

*Choose one responsibility you currently carry.*

Rewrite it as an outcome rather than a task. Then answer these questions:

1. What specifically changes or improves because I do this work well?
2. Where in my current role am I solving assigned problems only — and where could I be solving unassigned ones?
3. If someone were to describe my value to this organisation in two sentences, what would I want them to say — and does my current work support that?

*Titles describe position. Value defines influence. Choose to be valuable — and let the results speak.*

## Closing Reflection

Elena eventually understood what had happened.

She had been building a career around the title, assuming the authority it conferred would generate the trust she needed. David had been building something different — a quiet, consistent record of contribution that had accumulated, without announcement, into genuine influence.

Titles describe position.

**Value defines influence.**

In a changing workplace, those who focus on contribution remain relevant, trusted, and indispensable — not because they demanded recognition, but because they made it impossible to overlook.

Choose to be valuable.

**And let the results speak.**

The four chapters of Section III have been about how you grow. *Learning. Courage. Preparation. Value.* These are the capabilities that make consistent, visible contribution possible — the tools that turn intention into impact.

But capability without sustainability is a short story.

The final section asks the most important question of all: not how to grow, but how to keep going. How to protect your time, choose your standards, anchor your decisions in values, and finish what you start — not once, but over the full arc of a working life.

**That is the long game.**

SECTION IV

# THE LONG GAME

*How You Sustain*

CHAPTER

# TWELVE

## TIME IS A STRATEGIC ASSET

Grace was, by any external measure, extremely productive.

Her inbox was managed. Her meetings were attended. Her deliverables arrived on time. She was responsive, reliable, and present — the kind of professional that colleagues and managers depended on without thinking too hard about it, because she never gave them a reason to worry.

And yet, at the end of most weeks, she felt behind.

Not behind on tasks — those were done. Behind on the things that actually mattered to her. The strategic project she kept meaning to develop. The relationships she had been intending to invest in. The thinking she needed to do about where her career was going and what she wanted from the next five years.

Her days were full. Her direction was unclear.

The problem was not that Grace lacked time.

**The problem was that her time had no strategy.**

**Everyone receives the same twenty-four hours.**

What separates progress from frustration is not how much time you have, but how intentionally you use it. Time is often treated as something to fill, manage, or survive. Days become crowded, weeks blur together, and life begins to feel reactive rather than directed.

Yet time is not passive. It responds to priorities, boundaries, and the clarity with which you decide what deserves it.

When time is unmanaged, work feels rushed and exhausting.

**When time is intentional, progress feels calm and directional.**

## Time Reveals What Truly Matters

You do not need to explain your priorities.

**Your calendar already does.**

Where your time consistently goes is where your real priorities live — whether by conscious choice or by accumulated default. The meetings you accept without questioning. The interruptions you allow without cost. The tasks you postpone indefinitely. The requests you say yes to without considering what they displace.

All of it tells a story about what you have decided — consciously or not — matters most.

For many professionals, the honest review of a week's calendar is a clarifying and uncomfortable exercise. The things they care most about — their development, their most important relationships, their highest-value work — often occupy the smallest portion of their time. The things that simply arrived and demanded attention occupy the most.

**Awareness is the first step toward alignment.**

Until you see clearly how your time is actually being spent, you cannot redirect it meaningfully. The calendar review is not a productivity exercise. It is a values exercise.

## Time Requires Deliberate Protection

**Time that is not protected will be consumed.**

This is not a warning about bad intentions — most of what consumes unprotected time is entirely reasonable. Colleagues with genuine questions. Meetings that serve a real purpose. Requests from people you respect and want to help. The problem is not that these things are unreasonable. It is that they are unlimited, and your time is not.

Without deliberate protection, even the most important work is crowded out not by frivolity but by the accumulated weight of everything else's urgency.

Protecting time is not selfish.

**It is responsible.**

Strategic professionals decide in advance what deserves access to their time and what does not. They recognise that every yes carries a cost — the displacement of something else — and that every no preserves capacity for what genuinely matters. The discipline of saying no is not a failure of generosity. It is the condition under which meaningful contribution becomes possible.

## Time Multiplies When Used Intentionally

There is a counterintuitive quality to intentional time use: doing less, directed well, produces more than doing more, scattered widely.

When time aligns with purpose, effort feels lighter. Not because the work is easier, but because the energy behind it is not divided. Focus increases. Thinking deepens. Progress accelerates in ways that fragmented effort — spread across too many tasks, too many obligations, too many half-commitments — simply cannot replicate.

**Intentional time use turns hours into leverage.**

Small, consistent investments in the right direction produce returns that scattered effort never will. One focused hour on work that genuinely matters compounds differently than three distracted hours on work that simply arrived. Strategy transforms time from pressure into possibility.

## The Difference Between Busy and Effective

Busyness creates motion.

**Effectiveness creates movement.**

This distinction appeared at the very beginning of this book, in Chapter 1, with Marcus — the professional sitting at his desk at 9:47 on a Tuesday morning, fourteen messages waiting, six meetings ahead, feeling productive but unable to name a single thing he was building. His problem was not a lack of activity. It was a lack of direction.

The same dynamic plays out at the level of time. It is entirely possible to be active without advancing. A week can be full of tasks completed, emails answered, and meetings attended — and still leave you with the feeling that nothing important moved forward. That feeling is not imagined. It is the accurate perception of motion without direction.

Effectiveness asks a better question than "What did I do today?"

It asks: ***Is this moving me forward?***

When time is treated strategically, activity begins to serve direction rather than replace it. Grace's days were full. But until she asked that question honestly about where her time was going, they were full of motion rather than movement.

## Clarity Checkpoint

*Look honestly at last week's calendar — not the week you planned, but the one that actually happened.*

Then answer:

1. What does your actual time use reveal about your real priorities — as opposed to your stated ones?
2. What is one commitment that regularly consumes time without producing meaningful progress — and what would it cost to reduce or remove it?
3. Where in your week is there no protected time for your most important work? What would it take to create it?

*Time, when respected, works for you rather than against you. Treat it as the strategic asset it is.*

## Closing Reflection

Grace did not need more hours.

**She needed a different relationship with the ones she had.**

Time is neutral. It does not favour the ambitious or punish the distracted. It simply passes — and what you built with it, or failed to, becomes the record of how you spent a professional life.

Treat time as the strategic asset it is. Protect it deliberately, use it intentionally, and direct it toward what genuinely matters. When you do, progress becomes steadier, decisions feel lighter, and the long game becomes something you can actually sustain.

**Time, when respected, works for you rather than against you.**

CHAPTER

# THIRTEEN

## EXCELLENCE IS A CHOICE

The report was good enough.

Kwame knew it the moment he finished the first draft. It answered the question it was asked. The structure was logical. The data was accurate. Nobody who read it would have cause to complain.

He also knew it was not the best version of it he could produce.

Nobody would know the difference. The deadline was not pressing. There was other work waiting. Every practical argument pointed toward sending it as written.

He spent another forty minutes on it anyway.

He sharpened the executive summary until the argument was genuinely clear. He caught three places where a reader might lose the thread and restructured them. He added a paragraph anticipating the most likely question and answering it before it was asked.

When the report landed, the response was notably different from his usual work. Not because the topic was more important. Because the care was more visible.

Kwame had made a choice that nobody required of him.

**That is almost always where excellence begins.**

**Excellence is often admired from a distance.**

People point to it as something rare — a product of exceptional talent, fortunate circumstance, or a kind of innate drive that most people simply do not possess. From a distance, excellence looks like a trait. Up close, it looks like a series of small decisions.

**Excellence is a choice.**

It is chosen quietly, in decisions made daily about preparation, attention, and care. About whether something is done merely to completion or done well. About whether "good enough" is genuinely enough, or whether it is simply the point at which effort felt like it could stop.

Excellence is not about being better than others.

**It is about being intentional with what you produce.**

## Excellence Begins With Standards

Every outcome reflects a standard.

Most of the time, that standard was never consciously set. It was inherited from the environment, shaped by what colleagues accepted as normal, calibrated against what previous managers rewarded or ignored. Standards that are never deliberately chosen tend to drift toward the minimum that avoids negative consequence — which is a different thing entirely from the level that produces excellent work.

**Excellence begins when you make a deliberate decision about the level of quality you are willing to stand behind.**

Not a standard imposed by others. Not the minimum that satisfies expectations. A standard you have chosen because it reflects who you are choosing to become — a direct expression of the identity we explored in Chapter 4.

When standards are set deliberately and held consistently, behaviour adjusts to match them. Not through force, but through the internal pull of someone who has decided what their work represents.

## Excellence Shows in the Details

Excellence rarely announces itself.

It appears in the preparation done before the meeting — the homework that makes your contribution more considered than anyone expected. In the clarity applied before communication — the extra pass that removes ambiguity and respects the reader's time. In the follow-through after responsibility has been assigned — the update sent without being asked, the commitment honoured without needing a reminder.

**Details reveal values.**

They show how seriously you take the work, the process, and the people it affects. When someone pays attention to details that others overlook, the message is unmistakable: this person cares. And care, sustained over time, is one of the most reliable signals of excellence — because it cannot be faked consistently.

Trust grows quietly, detail by detail, in the minds of people who experience the difference.

## Excellence Builds Credibility Over Time

Credibility is not built through occasional brilliance.

A single excellent piece of work creates an impression. Consistent excellent work creates a reputation. And reputation — as Chapter 11 explored in the context of value — is the durable currency of professional influence. People come to rely on those who deliver quality regularly. Not perfectly, but dependably.

**Excellence compounds.**

Each piece of work done well adds to an accumulating record. Over time, that record becomes the first thing people think of when your name comes up in a room. Not the one time you were exceptional, but the pattern of consistent quality that makes you someone others want on their most important work.

## Excellence Does Not Require Perfection

Excellence and perfection are frequently confused.

They are not the same thing, and conflating them is expensive.

Perfection demands flawlessness.

**Excellence demands intention.**

Perfection is a standard that cannot, in practice, be met — which means it does not function as a standard at all. It functions as a reason to delay, to withhold, to revise endlessly without finishing. We saw this in Chapter 7, where perfectionism was named for what it often is: not high standards, but fear wearing a more respectable disguise.

Excellence, by contrast, is a standard that can be met. It does not require the absence of all imperfection. It requires the presence of genuine intention, careful effort, and honest engagement with the work. When the goal is excellence, improvement is continuous and pressure is manageable. When the goal is perfection, effort stalls at the edge of the impossible.

Excellence invites growth.

**Perfection resists it.**

## Choosing Excellence in Ordinary Moments

Excellence is not reserved for visible moments.

The choice Kwame made — to spend forty more minutes on a report that nobody required him to improve — is the kind of choice that forms the actual substance of an excellent career. Not the high-visibility moments, though those matter. The ordinary ones, the ones made without audience or applause, when good enough is genuinely available as an option and the person chooses better anyway.

This connects directly to what Chapter 6 named as discipline: the decision to honour your commitments to yourself, even when no one is watching. Excellence practiced in private is the same principle at the level of quality — not performing for others, but holding yourself to a standard because it reflects who you are.

Those ordinary moments shape habits.

Habits shape outcomes.

**And excellence practiced consistently, in the unglamorous dailiness of ordinary work, becomes something deeper than a behaviour. It becomes part of identity.**

## Clarity Checkpoint

*Choose one responsibility you handle regularly — one where "good enough" has become the default.*

Then answer honestly:

1. What would "excellent" specifically look like for this responsibility — not perfect, but genuinely excellent?
2. What is the gap between the standard I currently apply and the one I would be proud to apply?
3. Where have I been using the pursuit of perfection as a reason not to finish, rather than excellence as a reason to care?

*Excellence is not an event. It is a pattern. And patterns are built through choices repeated over time.*

## Closing Reflection

Nobody required Kwame's extra forty minutes.

**That is precisely what made them matter.**

Excellence is not an event.

**It is a pattern.**

And patterns are built through choices repeated over time — in the visible moments and the invisible ones, in the work that earns recognition and the work that simply needs doing well.

Choose excellence not as pressure, but as intention.

**Over time, it becomes your quiet signature.**

# CHAPTER FOURTEEN

## VALUES GUIDE DECISIONS

The offer was attractive. More than attractive.

Nadia had been approached about a senior role at a competitor. Better title, significantly higher compensation, a larger team. The people who contacted her were impressive. The organisation had momentum. On every practical measure, it made sense to move.

But there was something else.

Her current organisation was in the middle of a difficult transition. Her team — people she had hired, developed, and built trust with over three years — was navigating genuine uncertainty. She had told them, explicitly, that she was committed to seeing it through. Not as a formality. As a promise.

She spent two weeks in the decision. She talked it through with people she trusted. She ran the numbers. She imagined herself in the new role, in a year's time, having taken it.

And then she asked herself the question that had been underneath all the others:

> *"What kind of person do I want to be when I look back on this?"*

She declined the offer.

Not because the opportunity was wrong. But because leaving now would have been inconsistent with the person she had decided to be. And she had learned, over years, that the decisions that erode who you are cost more in the long run than the opportunities you decline.

**Decision-making becomes exhausting when values are unclear.**

Every choice feels heavy. Every option competes for attention. Every situation requires its own debate from first principles, because there is no settled internal compass to consult.

**But when values are clear, decisions simplify.**

Values act as internal anchors. They steady you when pressure rises, when emotions run high, and when urgency threatens to override wisdom. They do not make difficult decisions easy — but they make the basis for decisions clear. In a fast-moving world, that clarity is one of the most sustainable professional advantages available.

## Why Values Matter More Under Pressure

Pressure reveals priorities.

In calm moments, it is easy to speak about values. It costs nothing to name integrity, commitment, or care as important when nothing is demanding otherwise. The real test arrives when something is at stake — when the honest answer is inconvenient, when keeping a commitment has a visible cost, when the easier path and the right path diverge.

Without clear values, decisions made under pressure tend to default to fear, convenience, or the desire for approval — not because the person is weak, but because there is no settled compass to override those pulls in the moment.

**With clear values, the decision — even when difficult — has a foundation.**

Nadia's decision was not easy. But it was not confusing. She knew what she valued. That knowledge did not remove the difficulty of the choice. It removed the ambiguity.

**Values help you choose not just what is effective, but what is right.**

## Values Reduce Decision Fatigue

Many professionals experience decision fatigue not because they face too many decisions, but because they face the same kinds of decisions repeatedly — without a framework that resolves them.

When values are undefined, every choice requires fresh evaluation. Should I take this on? Should I speak up here? Should I compromise this, or hold the line? Each question demands energy. Over time, the cumulative weight of constant deliberation drains the clarity and confidence needed for the decisions that actually matter.

**Values simplify thinking by filtering options before emotion intervenes.**

When you know what matters most — genuinely, not just theoretically — many decisions resolve themselves before they become draining. The answer is not calculated fresh each time. It is already known. The energy saved is available for the work itself.

## Values Create Internal Alignment

Alignment occurs when actions reflect convictions.

When your decisions consistently align with your values, something quietly shifts in the experience of work. Effort feels lighter — not because the work is easier, but because there is no internal friction between what you are doing and who you are. You are not constantly negotiating with yourself, justifying choices that feel slightly off, or carrying the low-grade exhaustion of acting against your own convictions.

**Integrity replaces inner conflict.**

This internal alignment is also the foundation of the self-trust we explored in Chapter 6. When you can be relied upon by yourself — when your actions are consistently congruent with what you say you believe — confidence stops depending on external validation. It becomes something quieter and more stable: the knowledge that you are the same person in private that you are in public.

Values-aligned decisions do not just feel better. They compound into a kind of professional integrity that others sense, over time, without being able to fully name it.

## Values Shape Reputation and Legacy

Outcomes change.

Roles evolve.

Recognition fades.

**Values remain.**

Over a long career, people forget specific achievements far more readily than they forget how you made decisions, how you treated the people around you, and what you consistently stood for when things were difficult. Results are remembered briefly. Character is remembered long.

**This is what legacy actually means in professional life.**

Not the projects delivered or the targets hit — though those matter in their season. Legacy is the lasting impression left in the minds and experiences of the people you worked with, led, learned from, and served. It is built not through a single defining act but through the accumulation of value-driven choices made across an entire working life.

**Legacy is built through repeated value-driven choices.**

## Clarifying Your Core Values

Values do not need to be many to be effective.

A long list of values is often less useful than a short list held seriously. When everything is valued, nothing is prioritised. What creates clarity is not comprehensiveness but honesty — the willingness to name, with real specificity, the two or three things you are genuinely not willing to compromise, and then to apply them consistently enough that they become the lens through which decisions are made.

**A few well-defined values, applied consistently, provide more navigational clarity than a long list rarely referenced.**

The question to sit with is not "what do I believe?" — most professionals can answer that readily. The more demanding question is: "What do my actual decisions, under pressure, reveal that I believe?" That gap, where it exists, is where the work of values clarification is most needed and most productive.

**Values gain strength through application, not declaration.**

## Clarity Checkpoint

*Identify one core value you believe you hold — something you would name without hesitation if asked what matters most to you.*

Then answer honestly:

1. What does this value look like in practice — not as a statement, but as a specific observable behaviour?
2. Think of a recent decision made under pressure. Did my actual choice reflect this value — or did I compromise it?
3. Is there a current decision I am avoiding or delaying because the values-aligned answer is uncomfortable?

*Values become powerful when they are practised, not just stated. Let them guide your next decision — especially the difficult one.*

## Closing Reflection

Nadia did not regret her decision.

Not because the opportunity she declined was unworthy. But because the decision she made was congruent with the person she had been building, slowly and deliberately, across a long career. The cost was real. The integrity was worth it.

Values do not restrict freedom.

**They protect it.**

They free you from the constant uncertainty of decisions made without an anchor. They protect you from the slow erosion of a career built on choices that felt convenient at the time but accumulated into a life that did not quite match the person you intended to be.

In a world that moves quickly and rewards shortcuts, values remind you that *how* you choose matters as much as *what* you achieve.

Let your values guide your decisions.

**They will sustain you for the long game.**

CHAPTER

# FIFTEEN

## FINISH STRONG

Beginnings attract attention.
Endings reveal character.

You have reached the final chapter of this book. That matters. Not because finishing a book is a great achievement, but because the act of reaching the end of something — of not letting it drift into the category of things begun and quietly set aside — is already a small demonstration of what this chapter is about.

Many people start with enthusiasm. Goals are set, plans are made, energy is present. But as time passes and the novelty of beginning fades, follow-through weakens. The task lingers. The commitment drifts. The momentum that felt inevitable at the start dissipates quietly into the ordinary demands of ordinary days.

**Yet how you finish often matters more than how you start.**

Finishing is not merely about closure.

**It is about integrity.**

## Why Finishing Matters

Finishing reinforces the most important kind of discipline.

Each completed responsibility sends a signal — not to others, but to yourself — that you can be trusted to follow through. That signal is the same one Chapter 5 identified as the foundation of self-trust: the quiet accumulation of evidence that you are someone who does what they say they will do. Finishing is that principle applied not just to daily habits, but to the larger commitments that define a season, a project, a career.

Unfinished work, on the other hand, carries a weight that most people underestimate.

It occupies mental space long after active effort has stopped. It drains a low but constant trickle of energy — the background hum of things that are not done, commitments that are not met, loops that are not closed. Over time, the accumulation of unfinished things quietly erodes the sense of forward motion that makes sustained effort feel worthwhile.

Completion brings relief.

**And something more than relief. It brings strength.**

## Finishing Builds Momentum

Momentum does not come only from starting new things.

**It comes from closing loops.**

The professional who has ten things underway and none of them complete carries the friction of ten open threads. The one who completes one thing fully before beginning the next moves with a different quality of forward motion — lighter, cleaner, unburdened by the weight of accumulating incompleteness.

Each finished task reduces resistance to the next one. Progress feels achievable when work is completed rather than accumulated. And crucially — each finish provides the evidence of capability that Chapter 7 identified as the true source of confidence: not the feeling that precedes action, but the record that follows it.

**Finishing clears the path forward.**

## Finishing Reinforces Trust

People trust those who finish.

Not those who start impressively. Not those who commit enthusiastically. Those who complete.

Reliability is built through follow-through, not intention. The gap between what people say they will do and what they actually do is, in most organisations, surprisingly wide. The professional who closes that gap consistently — who delivers what was promised, when it was promised, without needing to be chased — builds a reputation that is quietly rare and quietly powerful.

**Trust, once established through consistent follow-through, opens doors that effort, talent, and even preparation alone cannot.**

## Finishing Shapes Identity

Finishers see themselves differently.

Each completed commitment reinforces an internal identity — the same identity Chapter 4 described as the foundation of lasting behaviour: *I am someone who follows through.* Over time, and through repetition, that identity becomes self-sustaining. Finishing stops feeling like an act of will and begins to feel like an expression of character.

**This is the long arc of everything this book has explored.**

Clarity about who you are and what matters. Consistency in how you show up. Capability built through learning, courage, and preparation. And now, at the end, the sustained commitment to finishing what you start — not occasionally, not when conditions are favourable, but as the defining pattern of how you operate across a whole working life.

**Identity is shaped not only by what you start, but by what you complete.**

## Finishing in Seasons, Not Just Tasks

The discipline of finishing extends beyond individual tasks.

Careers unfold in seasons. There are seasons of building and seasons of delivering. Seasons of learning and seasons of leading. Seasons of starting things and seasons of completing them. One of the marks of professional maturity is the ability to recognise which season you are in — and to finish it well, rather than drifting out of it sideways.

**Finishing a season intentionally means closing it with care.**

Completing the commitments made within it. Leaving what you built in a condition that others can continue. Acknowledging what was learned and what was hard. Releasing what is being left behind without resentment or regret, so that the energy needed for the next season arrives clean rather than encumbered.

Strong finishes do more than close chapters. They create the space, restore the energy, and rebuild the momentum that new beginnings require.

**Every good beginning is made possible by a good ending.**

## A Final Clarity Checkpoint

*This final checkpoint is different from the others.*

Rather than focusing on a single task or habit, look back across the whole of what you have read.

**Which chapter landed hardest?**

The one where you felt recognised — where something named a pattern you live with but have not previously named clearly. That chapter is likely where your most immediate work lies.

**Which chapter did you resist?**

The one you read quickly, or found reasons to set aside. Resistance is often the mind's way of protecting something it is not yet ready to change. That chapter deserves a second reading.

**And finally: what is the one thing you will do differently this week?**

Not fourteen things. One. The smallest, most specific action that moves in the direction of who you are choosing to become.

## Closing Reflection

Across fifteen chapters, we have followed people who were not extraordinary.

They were professionals navigating ordinary circumstances — too many meetings, unclear direction, feedback that stung, opportunities that felt just out of reach, the daily accumulation of decisions made under pressure with incomplete information. They were not gifted with unusual talent or unusually favourable conditions. They were simply people who chose, in specific moments, to be more intentional than the situation required.

**That is the whole argument of this book.**

Clarity gives direction. Consistency builds momentum. Capability grows through learning, courage, and the willingness to prepare seriously and contribute visibly. And values — lived faithfully, under pressure, in the decisions that cost something — sustain everything else across the full arc of a working life.

None of this requires perfection.

**It requires intention.**

The long game is not won in a single brilliant moment. It is built in the ordinary ones — in the quiet decisions made when no one is watching, in the habits maintained when motivation has faded, in the standards held when good enough was genuinely available and excellence was chosen anyway.

You have reached the end of this book.

**Now finish the work it pointed toward.**

Finish strong.

**And step into what comes next with confidence.**

# A BIBLIOGRAPHIC NOTE

## This book does not belong to the productivity tradition.

It does not offer systems, workflows, or frameworks for doing more faster. Its argument is the opposite: that most professionals already have the capacity they need, and that the gap between where they are and where they want to be is rarely a systems gap. It is an identity gap. A clarity gap. A gap between what they value and what their daily decisions reveal they actually prioritise.

The books listed here are the ones that most shaped the thinking behind these pages. Some are direct intellectual ancestors. Others are included because they represent the conversation this book is joining — and in some cases, the conversation it is gently pushing back on. Readers who want to go deeper on any of the book's four themes will find each section a genuine starting point rather than a reading list assembled for appearance.

The annotations are personal. They explain not just what each book argues but why it belongs here.

### SECTION I: CLARITY — THE INNER LIFE OF WORK

Frankl, Viktor E.. *Man's Search for Meaning*. Beacon Press, 1959.

The foundational argument that meaning precedes motivation — that human beings can endure almost any how if they have a sufficient why. Chapter 2's argument about purpose as a focus mechanism draws directly on Frankl's insight that clarity of meaning is not a luxury but a navigational necessity. Required reading for anyone who has ever felt productive but empty.

Aurelius, Marcus. *Meditations.* Various editions (written c. 161–180 CE), .

The original daily practice of intentional self-examination. What is striking about the Meditations is not the philosophy but the method: a working leader returning, every day, to the same questions about what he values and how he is living. The practice of clarity described in Chapter 1 is a direct descendant of this tradition. Aurelius did not write these notes for publication. He wrote them because he needed them.

Newport, Cal. *Deep Work: Rules for Focused Success in a Distracted World.* Grand Central Publishing, 2016.

Newport's case that the ability to perform cognitively demanding work without distraction is becoming both rarer and more valuable is well-made and well-evidenced. This book departs from his emphasis on systems and rules, arguing that depth is a product of clarity and identity rather than scheduling discipline alone. But the underlying diagnosis — that most professional environments actively work against the conditions needed for excellent work — is one this book shares fully.

Brooks, David. *The Second Mountain: The Quest for a Moral Life.* Random House, 2019.

The distinction Brooks draws between résumé virtues and eulogy virtues maps closely onto the values and legacy arguments in Chapters 13 and 14. His observation that many successful professionals reach the top of the first mountain and find it oddly unsatisfying — because they optimised for the wrong things — is the subtext of several chapters in this book. Particularly relevant to mid-career readers.

McKeown, Greg. *Essentialism: The Disciplined Pursuit of Less.* Crown Business, 2014.

The clearest articulation of the idea that almost everything is non-essential, and that the ability to identify and protect what is genuinely important is a skill that must be cultivated deliberately. Chapter 2's argument about purpose as a filter for what deserves attention, and Chapter 12's treatment of time as a strategic asset, both draw on the essentialist logic McKeown develops here.

## Section II: Consistency — The Daily Practice of Showing Up

Clear, James. *Atomic Habits: An Easy and Proven Way to Build Good Habits and Break Bad Ones.* Avery, 2018.

The most rigorous recent treatment of habit formation, and the book this one most consciously builds on and departs from. Clear's insight that identity-based habits are more durable than outcome-based ones is the foundation of Chapter 4. Where this book differs is in its emphasis on the internal work that must precede the systems: you cannot architect your way to identity. Chapter 4's James is the person who tried Clear's system without first doing the identity work, and found it insufficient.

Duckworth, Angela. *Grit: The Power of Passion and Perseverance.* Scribner, 2016.

Duckworth's research on sustained effort as a better predictor of long-term performance than talent is the empirical backbone of the consistency section. Her finding that grit — the combination of passion and perseverance for long-term goals — can be developed rather than simply possessed connects directly to Chapter 6's argument about discipline as a chosen posture rather than an inherited trait.

Holiday, Ryan. *Ego Is the Enemy.* Portfolio/Penguin, 2016.

The Stoic professional tradition at its most directly applicable. Holiday's argument that ego — the need for recognition, the attachment to a self-image that must be protected — is the most reliable source of professional self-sabotage connects to multiple chapters in this book, particularly Chapter 3 on mindset and Chapter 11 on value versus title. The person who confuses the map for the territory, who values the credential over the capability it is supposed to represent, is a recurring figure in Holiday's work and in these pages.

Irvine, William B.. *A Guide to the Good Life: The Ancient Art of Stoic Joy.* Oxford University Press, 2008.

The most accessible contemporary introduction to Stoic philosophy as a practical framework for professional and personal life. Irvine's treatment of the dichotomy of control — focusing energy on what you can influence and releasing what you cannot — is directly relevant to Chapters 5 and 6. The relationship between self-discipline and self-respect that gives Chapter 6 its title has deep roots in the Stoic tradition Irvine describes.

## Section III: Capability — Growing Into What You Can Become

Dweck, Carol S.. *Mindset: The New Psychology of Success.* Random House, 2006.

The research foundation for Chapter 3. Dweck's distinction between fixed and growth mindsets — between the belief that ability is innate and the belief that it can be developed through effort — is now widely cited, but the original work remains the most precise and evidence-based articulation of it. The specific mechanism by which fixed-mindset beliefs lead to avoidance and growth-mindset beliefs lead to engagement is what Chapter 3 is describing from the inside.

Coyle, Daniel. *The Talent Code: Greatness Isn't Born. It's Grown. Here's How.*. Bantam Books, 2009.

Coyle's investigation into how high performance is actually built — through deep practice, ignition, and master coaching — provides the neurological grounding for the book's argument that capability is grown, not given. Chapter 8's distinction between accumulating information and applying it intentionally maps directly onto Coyle's concept of deep practice: the uncomfortable, targeted effort at the edges of current ability that produces genuine skill development.

Godin, Seth. *Linchpin: Are You Indispensable?*. Portfolio/Penguin, 2010.

The argument that the most durable professional advantage is not compliance or credential but genuine, irreplaceable contribution. Chapter 11's distinction between value and title — and the observation that organisations increasingly reward those who make things better rather than those who simply hold a role — is the same argument Godin makes through the lens of creative economy. Elena and David's story in Chapter 11 is a direct dramatisation of Godin's thesis.

Crawford, Matthew B.. *Shop Class as Soulcraft: An Inquiry into the Value of Work.* Penguin Press, 2009.

A philosophical defence of excellent work done with genuine care and practical mastery. Crawford's argument that there is a particular kind of satisfaction available only through work that is done well — that resists shortcuts, that requires real engagement with resistant material — is the philosophical foundation beneath Chapter 13's treatment of excellence. The distinction between doing something to completion and doing it well is exactly the distinction Crawford is exploring throughout this book.

Brown, Brené. *Dare to Lead: Brave Work. Tough Conversations. Whole Hearts.*. Random House, 2018.

Brown's research on vulnerability, courage, and values-based leadership informs Chapter 9's treatment of professional courage and Chapter 14's argument about values under pressure. Her finding that courage is a learnable practice rather than a personality trait — and that the willingness to be seen trying, and possibly failing, is a professional skill that can be deliberately developed — is the empirical grounding for Chapter 9's argument.

## SECTION IV: THE LONG GAME — SUSTAINING WHAT YOU HAVE BUILT

Drucker, Peter F.. *The Effective Executive: The Definitive Guide to Getting the Right Things Done.* HarperCollins, 1966.

Sixty years old and still the most precise treatment of effectiveness as distinct from efficiency. Drucker's central observation — that the question is never how to do things right but how to find the right things to do — is the engine of Chapter 12's argument about busyness versus effectiveness. Grace's problem in Chapter 12 is the problem Drucker identified in 1966: a professional whose days are full of activity that does not add up to progress.

Holiday, Ryan. *The Obstacle Is the Way: The Timeless Art of Turning Trials into Triumph.* Portfolio/Penguin, 2014.

Holiday's earlier book on the Stoic discipline of reframing adversity as material for growth. The argument that circumstances are not the constraint — that the response to circumstances is where character is built and capability developed — runs as a thread through the Long Game section. Particularly relevant to Chapter 9's treatment of courage and Chapter 15's argument about finishing seasons with integrity rather than resentment.

Covey, Stephen R.. *The 7 Habits of Highly Effective People.* Free Press, 1989.

Included not because this book resembles it — the approaches are meaningfully different — but because any honest bibliography of work in this tradition must acknowledge the book that defined the genre. Covey's principle-centred framework, and in particular his distinction between urgent and important, remains one of the most widely distributed frameworks in professional development. This book begins where Covey's begins: with the inner life as the foundation of the outer. It parts ways in insisting that the inner work cannot be shortcut by principles alone.

Frankl, Viktor E.. *Man's Search for Meaning.* Beacon Press, 1959.

Listed again in this final section because Frankl belongs here as much as at the beginning. His argument that the last of human freedoms is the freedom to choose one's response to any given circumstance — that between stimulus and response there is always a space, and in that space lies our power — is the deepest foundation of Chapter 14's values argument and Chapter 15's closing. The long game is ultimately about that space: what you do with it, consistently, over the full arc of a working life.

## A Final Note

**Books do not change behaviour. People do.**

The books listed here are invitations to think more carefully, not instructions to follow more faithfully. Every thinker represented here would say the same. The work they point toward is not the reading. It is what happens after.

Return to this list when a chapter resonated and you want to go deeper. Return to it when a chapter challenged you and you want to push back.

The conversation these writers are having with each other, and with you, is more valuable than any single book in it — including this one.

## Connect with the Author

books.by/lanre-b-olaleye | lanrebolaleye.com

LinkedIn: Insight with LBO | apexcareer.ai.

www.ingramcontent.com/pod-product-compliance
Lightning Source LLC
LaVergne TN
LVHW011029110826
845149LV00015B/3343
*9798995815006*